CCSS Genre Realistic Fi

MW00710116

Essential Question
How do animals survive?

An Arctic Life for Us

by Brian Hannigan

illustrated by CA Nobens

Chapter 1
Hot and Cold 2

Chapter 2
A Good Idea 6

Chapter 3
Maybe Not. 10

Chapter 4
Better Than Nothing 13

Respond to Reading 16

PAIRED READ What Is a Ptarmigan? 17

Focus on Genre 20

Hot and Cold

Marcos was tired of being hot. The summer days had been very long and very, very sunny. The temperature had climbed to over 100 degrees many times.

Today was another hot one.

"Mom," Marcos said as he walked into the kitchen, "I'm hot. Can we go to the library? It's always nice and cool inside, and I want to read about cold places. Maybe that will help me cool off."

"Sure," Mom said. "The library sounds like a good place to be this afternoon. We can go in just a few minutes."

Soon, Marcos and Mom walked through the doors of the library. Marcos smiled as the cool air hit his skin, and he blinked as his eyes got used to the dimmer light.

That's much better, he thought.

In the pleasant silence, Marcos searched for books about cold places. He found three books about the Arctic Circle and plopped down on a beanbag chair to look at the covers. On the first cover, polar bears walked over huge chunks of ice.

That looks nice, Marcos thought.

He opened the book and read about the polar bears. Their thick fur helped keep them warm even in the icy water. Their fur looked white in the sun and helped hide them in the white snow and ice.

In the next book, Marcos read about seals. They had a thick layer of fat to help them stay warm. Their sleek coats helped them slip through the water and across the ice.

That looks like fun, Marcos thought as he imagined the freedom of swimming and splashing in the chilly water.

CHAPTER 2

A Good Idea

Marcos smiled at the idea of living in the Arctic. He wondered if people actually lived there, so he looked in the index of the book in his hand. Yes, there was a section about people!

Marcos read that not a lot of people live in the Arctic. Perfect! Marcos thought.

We'll have plenty of room. It would be a great place for our family to live!

Marcos looked around, eager to find Mom. He found her nearby and rushed over to tell her his amazing plan.

"Mom!" Marcos said in a loud whisper, "I have a good idea for getting out of the heat! We can move to the Arctic!"

"Oh, we can?" Mom said, smiling.

"Yes, look at these pictures. Doesn't it look cool there?"

"Actually, it looks cold," Mom said.

Marcos was pretty sure Mom was trying not to laugh, so he quickly kept going.

"I'll bet Dad could get a job there. Maybe he could catch fish or run a dogsled business. I'm sure some kids live there, so you could still be a teacher."

"Mmm-hmm," Mom said. "That's an interesting idea, but..."

Marcos spoke quickly before she could say no. "You always say we should be out in the fresh air more. We'd have a lot of good, fresh, cold air there! We would be healthier! We could even live in an igloo. Look, here's a picture of one!"

Marcos turned to the page with a home made of ice. "Okay, well, people don't really live in igloos anymore, but it would still be fun to have one," he said.

CHAPTER 3

Maybe Not

"Honey, I'm sure the Arctic would be an amazing place to live, but that's a very cold climate. It's too cold for us, I'm afraid. We're not used to that kind of weather."

"We could adapt, just like the animals do!" Marcos said. "We could wear thick coats and boots. We could dye our hair white so we could have white fur like the animals! We'd blend right in. Come on, Mom, where's your sense of adventure?"

Now Mom really did laugh. She patted Marcos on the cheek and said, "Come on, it's time to go home. If you want to check those books out, go take them to the counter."

Marcos stopped talking. He unhappily picked up his books and took them to the librarian. He waited while she checked them out for him. Then he walked slowly to the car.

"Don't be sad," Mom said. "I know it's been a hot summer, but it will be fall soon. The weather will cool off, school will start, and you'll see all your friends."

Marcos nodded, but the car was hot, and he was too.

CHAPTER 4

Better Than Nothing

At home, Marcos took his books to his room. He reread the pages about the seals slipping across the ice.

He thought about the long hall outside his room. He thought about what he could do to make himself as slippery as a seal.

Marcos dug to the bottom of his dresser drawer and pulled out a pair of fuzzy winter pajamas. He put them on over his clothes, rushed to the hall, ran, and slid on his stomach.

13

It worked, sort of. He did hit the floor with a thud, and he didn't really go very far, but for a moment he felt like a seal!

Mom stuck her head around the corner to ask, "What was that noise?" When she walked into the hall, she saw Marcos on the floor wearing winter pajamas. "What are you doing?"

"I'm an Arctic seal sliding on the ice," Marcos said. Sweat was starting to drip down his face.

"You're a very hot, sweaty seal," Mom said. "If you really need to feel cool, put on your swimsuit. I'll take you to the pool."

"Hooray!" Marcos said.

It wasn't the Arctic, but it was better than nothing!

Respond to Reading

Summarize

Use important details to summarize *An Arctic Life for Us*. Information from the chart will help.

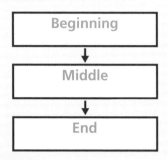

Text Evidence

1. How do you know that *An Arctic Life for Us* is realistic fiction? GENRE

2. What is the main character's goal in the story? Use details in the story to support your answer. PLOT

3. Use what you know about prefixes to figure out the meaning of *unhappily* on page 11. PREFIXES

4. Write about Marcos's plan and how he thinks the family can adapt. Use details from the story to help you. WRITE ABOUT READING

CCSS Genre Expository Text

Compare Texts

Read about an animal that adapts to its cold home.

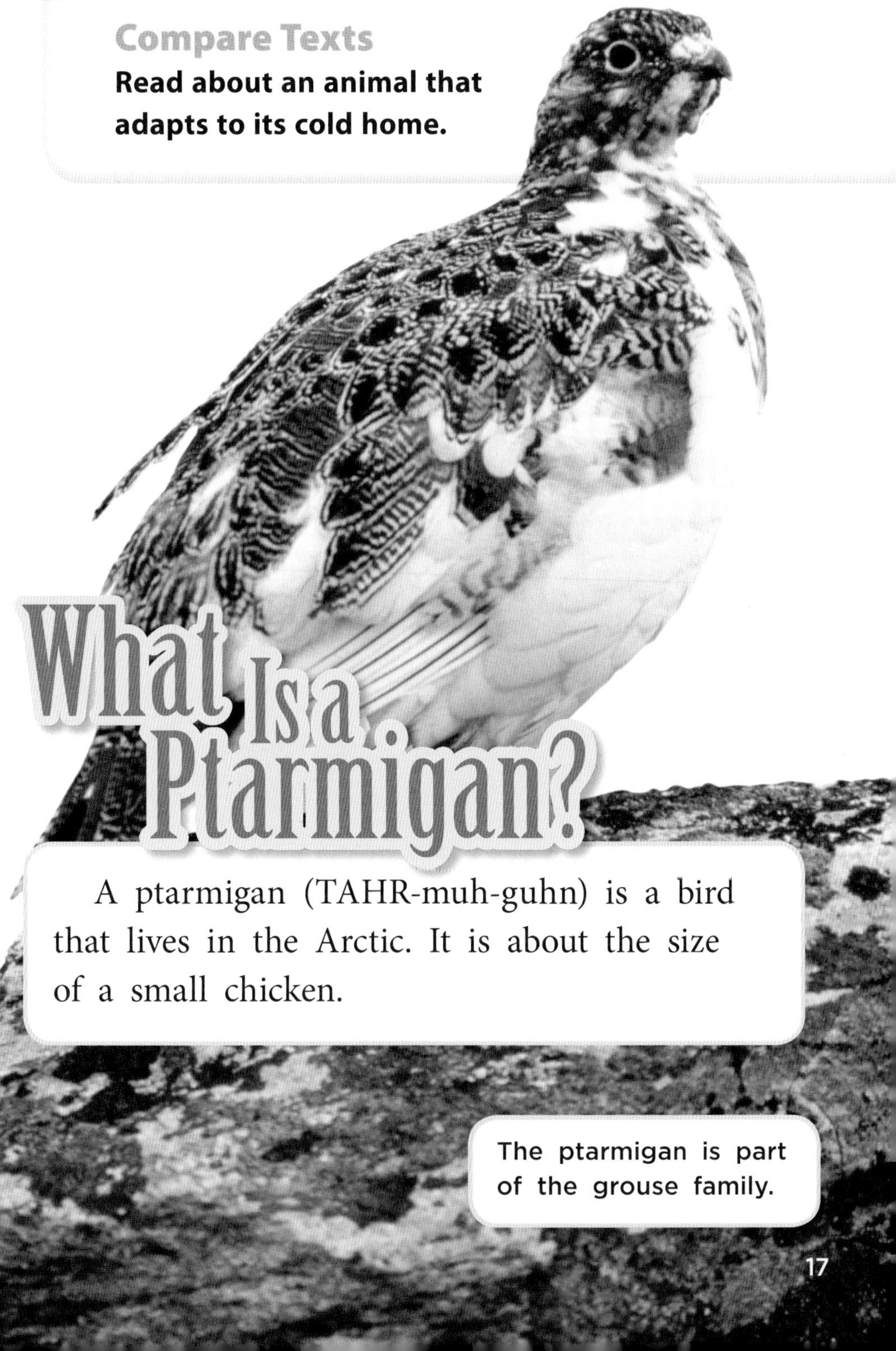

What Is a Ptarmigan?

A ptarmigan (TAHR-muh-guhn) is a bird that lives in the Arctic. It is about the size of a small chicken.

The ptarmigan is part of the grouse family.

In summer, the ptarmigan's feathers are gray and brown. The bird blends in with the tundra plants. The pattern on its feathers looks like shadows in the grass.

This is what a ptarmigan looks like in the summer.

Tom Brakefield/Stockbyte/Getty Images

In winter, the ptarmigan's feathers turn pure white. Now the bird blends in with the snow and ice. It can hide from enemies.

Ptarmigans do not migrate to warmer temperatures.

Make Connections

How do ptarmigans adapt? ESSENTIAL QUESTION

Is a ptarmigan a bird Marcos might have read about in his library books? Explain. TEXT TO TEXT

Focus on

Genre

Realistic Fiction Realistic fiction is a made-up story with events that could happen in real life. The people and places in the story seem like real people and places.

What to Look For Marcos and his mom in *An Arctic Life for Us* are like real people. They might be like people you know. The story happens in places that seem real. The events in the story, or the plot, are things that could happen in real life.

Your Turn

Write a realistic fiction story. Make a story map to outline your story. Include characters, setting, and plot. Be sure they are people, places, and events that could be real. Write a short description of each main character. Tell what happens in the beginning, middle, and end of the story. Write your story and share it with the class.